NEW YORK
POETS
SERIES

SPINOZA DOESN'T
COME HERE ANYMORE

SPINOZA DOESN'T
COME HERE ANYMORE
POEMS BY COLETTE INEZ

MELVILLE HOUSE
HOBOKEN, NEW JERSEY

Melville House Publishing
P.O. Box 3278
Hoboken, NJ 07030

Series editors: Valerie Merians and Dennis Loy Johnson
Design and photography: David Konopka

ISBN: 0-9749609-1-8

First Edition

Library of Congress Cataloging-in-Publication data on file.

AGAIN FOR SAUL

CONTENTS

SPINOZA DOESN'T COME HERE ANYMORE

.

SPINOZA DOESN'T COME HERE ANYMORE

Spinoza used to buy us chocolate doughnuts
at Donut Delight, shop for groceries
at Superette. Where has he gone?
He isn't here to look the other way
when slim-flanked coeds strut by
clothed by Lorette and Benetton.
A hardened bachelor in a neighborhood
of women eager to share a meal,
he'd eat a take-out mu shu
shrimp from Hunan North.
He'd sworn off Kosher foods
after the synagogue booted him out
for saying civic order is enhanced
by free thought.
Sometimes we'd see him hunched
over coffee at The Happy Burger.
He used to ask who is happy on Broadway?
He used to ask about ethics demonstrated
in the geometrical manner.
Often, he discussed primordial reality.
What is God? He wanted talk
that crackled and glowed like fireworks
over the Hudson on the Fourth of July.
When he posed the question:
what is the essence of mind,

nobody knew at Luggage and Gifts,
Foto Rush, Pizza Town's Restaurant,
Angela's Gourmet. Spinoza rarely
goes there. It is pointless to look.
We seek him out at Leroy's Pharmacy.
He takes more Bufferin than is good for him,
and his eyes are bad from grinding lenses
in the half light of his shop. No sign of him
at Bahama Mama's or Bit of Bengal
in the back booth where he'd study Descartes.
Spinoza? Someone spotted him at Avram's store,
Optimo Cigars. We remember he enjoys
an after dinner smoke, coughs too much,
shrugs off doctors, and carries on
about the infinitely infinite
productive machine that is the apprehended
universe, he says, at Hersh's Sportswear
to Hersh who gave up trying to persuade
his friend to look like someone dignified.
No one has seen him at the P.O.
shuffling on line in a black coat
and scuffed boots to buy foreign stamps.
He exchanges letters
with scholars worldwide.
Nothing comes from our search
at Health Nuts where he'd stock up

on eye lotions and lozenges,
herbal teas and brewer's yeast.
At Evita's Coffee Shop, Evita says right off,
"Spinoza doesn't come here anymore."
Where has he taken off
with his axioms and postulates,
his prefaces and appendices?
"He left this," she hands us a note which reads:
Dear Friends:

> *I've lost my lease on the store but have found*
> *new space in Hoboken.*
> *The divine spirit of the universe must be seen*
> *from the backdrop of eternity.*

> *Yours,*
> Baruch

COMO PANTOUM

The day I met Perry Como
General MacArthur had a parade.
I'd been given the afternoon off
from the office where I worked.

General MacArthur had a parade.
I could barely see through the crowd
in front of the office where I worked.
"Want a lift?" I heard a voice behind me.

I could barely see through the crowd.
Hands at my hips raised and held me.
"Want a lift?" I heard a voice behind me,
saw in a glance St. Patty's and Saks Fifth.

The hands that raised and held me
belonged to a hunk in a Brooks Brothers suit.
I saw Saks Fifth and St. Patty's at a glance.
"Would you like to meet Perry Como?" he asked.

This heartthrob in the Brooks Brothers suit
said he was in entertainment, a rep.
"Are you kidding, would I like to meet Perry Como?"
He said he knew Perry as a personal friend.

He told me he was in entertainment, a rep.
Today I can't remember his name.
"Are you kidding, would I like to meet Perry Como?"
At his studio Como sang *It's Impossible*.

Today I can't remember this guy's name.
I think he called once and we met for drinks.
At the TV studio Como sang *It's Impossible*
and General MacArthur had his parade.

I think that rep called once and we met for drinks,
but like an old soldier he just faded away.
I'll always remember the MacArthur parade
the day Como sang *It's Impossible.*

PRISON/CLOUDS

Passing the state correctional facility,
a gunner in the gun post.

Hard blue. After flat miles
of cotton, the prison tower startled.

A day of modest happiness marred,
him saying she's said something she hadn't.

Grim, she stares at clouds leaving islands
where they break apart.

Prisoners believe others
share the grace not to be penned in.

Witness to sunlight's captive colors,
released to the line between heaven and earth,

he ends the impasse: "I might have misheard."
Yield, said the road.

THE SKEPTIC

I am the free-thinker who reads Voltaire.
    A photograph of Karl Marx adorns my piano.
I quote from Robert Ingersoll's *Why I Am an Agnostic.*
    "I doubt therefore I am" never said by Pascal,
yet I am and I doubt any interpretation
    of god that doesn't also describe him as a symbolic
tribal father hurling biblical rancor at the nations.
    I doubt his alleged only son as anything more than a
dissident perched in fictive heaven
    among angels who sometimes fly down to earth
to keep drunks and debtors from jumping into rivers.
    I doubt celestial virgins will visit the men who ate
pizza in Florida, shopping smart at discount stores.
    Consigned to the zero of null, they are specks of ash
alongside those they killed in the name of their divinity.
I want to put an extra "O" between G O and D, I'll pray
to that: love, friends, music, books, reason and beauty.

ELIZABETH, THE RAIN

softens the earth where you've fallen
far beyond the talk
of souls becoming birds—
Elizabeth, which bird is yours?
Sand hill crane, high flyer, bright crow?

Is it they who have taken you away from me?
Or a sandpiper at the lip of the foam
where seabirds pray to rain
as another dominion of water?
Each day more souls fly in swarms

pulled by the sun and moon
above your stone—a green swell before the splash,
rainsoaked, distant grass
where clouds in flight console you,
but not the uproar in me at your leaving.

COURTYARD NOISES FROM THE NORTH, TWENTY FOURTH PRECINCT

A blasted horn, do do di do,
shenanigans, summer,
grunting apes on stereo.

The city lets out its seams,
burly clouds burst,
buckling thunder.

Monkey business in the cosmic skin,
somewhere a platter
of quiet light.

Put that in the horn
and pipe it.
Let the apes huff
all the way home

to Baboonis Majoris
in a mangrove of stars.
Blue-white Vega, red Antares,
what falls like a fringe of dust?

Illiterate silence
sealed under glass
like basalt from the moon.

STALKING ee IN THE FIFTIES

I knew him by his tonsure,
head bare as a Buddhist monk
or a bowl holding lower case letters

that poured out on a page.
I almost saw that spillage
running out of his hands as he unlatched

the gate of Patchin Place;
O, ee, I followed him down Sixth
in jacket weather, he, neatly made

and wearing tweed. At the bakery
he pointed to swirls of pastry. A baguette
poked out of his paper bag like a periscope.

I remember asters, mums at the florist. Purple, pink
peeped out of the wrappings.
In the deli would he pick

Genoese salami, sliced thin, my favorite,
or half-sour pickles, the color of lagoons
in Lamour, Hope, Crosby films?

Far from frangipani, ee turned towards Sixth,
his face a mask, and I followed like Old Dog Tray
pretending the letter I'd never mail:

Dear ee,

Your "Somewhere I have never traveled"
charts my realm, too, even as I step from here to there,
too moony by half to ask for your autograph.
I failed to say I lived with Roethke's "sadness of pencils"
in gray cubicles, carbon paper stains
on hands that itched to compose

more than shaky notes for poems after squabbling
with a lover, "glad and big."
Moaning through rooms of maybe and no,

I wanted the impertinence of Edward Estlin C, to tease
like him
a sort of antic beauty of words reckoned on the page.
O, ee I wanted to leave

my lip prints on the flap of an envelope
holding the poems I'd never send,
though I could have left them at your door,

you were that near
when I stalked you back then
in love with your line

                       s.

DAMP PARADISE
(Sweet Briar, Virginia)

Benignly drunk and barefoot, I danced on loose tiles.
A quince flower in my hair and in my garden of euphonious sounds:
soaked peonies succumbed to the blue thunder of drums.

Wasn't it the hour of rainbows spanning the lake?
Wasn't this how I let my breath escape little by little into
flesh-colored clouds?

I almost remember your hesitant voice, forget the silence
when you turned away. Here the path says nothing, not a word
to the rabbit apparition at the gravel's edge.

Sated with answered prayers for rain, bits of fur and straw
bunch together in stubborn mud. I fixate on the solstice rushing
past molecules of what was lost.

And how the Milky Way spread its haze through Cassiopeia's
starry chair. Now spring's damp heaven comes smudged,
braided with runnels and cracks in the road.

SONG FOR FERNAND LÉGER

Léger of Argentan in the parade
of mechanical whirs; motors & gears,
railways & tubes, furnaces & factories,
broke with the past.
Beguiled by the grim industrial towns,
he honored scaffolding & beams,
cylinders & slabs, smokestacks & signs,
stairwells & halls, columns & spheres.
Grids & scrolls, semi-abstract,
robot-like shapes leapt from the brush
of this proletarian who turned his back
on that grand parade of art
extolling the bourgeoisie. Yellow boomed
from his canvases, lines banded with black,
furious blues & reds stroking cool whites
through a fracture of forms, mechanical, semi-abstract,
in the dance of *la vie ordinaire,*

Léger, mon frére, like you I've thumbed my nose
at the past, at my prie-dieu, at the chiaroscuro garb
of our nuns, their lips brushing cups
of sacramental wine.
I have painted in imagination the milkman's
coat gray white as the doctor who took my pulse,
advising oranges for a fevered throat.

I have thought to paint a faint purple line
between tan stubble & soot-colored sky.
When an iron beast hooted smoke across a field,
I saw the furious red sun blazing through haze,
& hid my head in the wing of my arm
all before the grand parade of art gave me consent
to march with you to the bugle & fife,
the cymbal & drum of la vie extraordinaire.

TWO KASHMIRI POETS

To prepare an introduction
to Agha Shahid Ali's *A Nostalgist's Map of America*
his childhood friend, Rafique, positions gray arrows and loops
from one page to another, littering signals
of emphasis and joy.

Eloquent fire transmuted to colors of ash,
his pencil's flourish logs phrases with a slash,
check marks, underlines images of water, themes of death
and stars. Circled words *night, loss, silence, rain.*
"Rich in thought," Rafique plays his wit in modest print

alongside Agha's "I spoke like a poor man..."
from "Beyond the Ash Rains."
Inhabiting silences between strophes,
Rafique will also brood on the sorrow
of a nephew killed with the Mujahadeen in Afghanistan.

Rafique may start his poem with an image of fighter planes
buzzing the Himalayas. Perhaps the Yeti he invents
will cover its ears as it runs for cover.
To these exiled poets of bitter roads
diverging in the mountains, there is the question of longing

for the wholeness of one's country.
Lessons from Srinagar spin stories:

Mughal gardens, a glitter to summon in a feast of talk
that embraces translations from the Urdu
of Ghalib and Faiz in Amherst and New York.

SPRING OFFENSIVE

Even as scientists map the human genome,
measure the universe to clock the Big Bang,

resonating barks in our galaxy of back
apartments call us to the window.

Skirmishes between the dogs in our courtyard.
Spring drives back winter, assault of rain clouds.

Red-eyed Taurus in the pit bulls's glare, blood
roses for the maimed fox terrier.

The Pekinese yips for the lap of its praise giver,
convoys of canine owners wend home from the park.

We quarrel over a bone of inconsequence,
ancestral echoes of contention.

After the squall April constellations appear
too fragile to decode above a purple blur.

Black holes collide in a point of space-time
so dense light cannot escape.

If Einstein is right, they are pockets
of tremendous mass.

But things don't exist until found.
The weakness of our position isn't news

nor the spring sky in a time of war
nor war about to erupt, more or less real

like the deeply-throated bark of the Dog Star
too far off to imagine.

MY PRIEST FATHER'S

. . . V-necked, tobacco-colored cardigan pocked with tiny holes
burned by embers of his cigarettes.
He wore it when he'd flung off his collar in the sacristy.

I believe he preferred the beauty of women to the virtue
of sermons. I believe he preferred their beauty to giving
absolution.

A gift from his mother who favored him
in uniform: lieutenant-at-arms in the militant church.
He slipped the sweater on and off during those years

before he met my handsome mother in her smoke-colored dress.
When I mull on him naked, nothing but mystery colors my view,
to think I've seen nothing of him but one photographed face,

the body that made me stripped under earth where he wears
the western light of stars.

COLD MONTAGE

kleenex   antihistamines   oranges

inhalants   sucrets   wintergreen   lozenges

flannel gown buttoned to the neck   hachoo

mail read in a blur vapor rub   advil blue

snow   phlegm-colored sun   drowsy stars sheep-

counting Lalo Lully lull me to sleep

soul to wake to blahs broth green tea

Poulenc   Bizet   Chopin   Satie

RESCUE AND RETURN

Behind me, sand castles under siege,
    foundering in foam. Hard to say how I swam so far.

I wanted to be salvaged, wanted to be drowned.
    Phlegm and seawater clogged my lungs.

In a half dream, ghostly as opalescent nudibranch
    or secretions of milt, I hitched a ride home

where corn and lima beans
    glistened in pots. I was late again for supper.

Grandma's eyes dimmed in the incoming storm of her quarrel.
    I imagined rain and lightning like long-legged birds

careening through dunes.
    The next day promised a lift to the beach.

Grim-lipped Grandma shouted "Only floozies wear
    shorts that short."

My ride pulled up in a red MG and I turned fifteen.
    Past the West Bath House, another rise

of waves, and I dove through their green transparent doors.

AFTER MAMELEH LEAPT OUT THE WINDOW,
HER FURNITURE WENT TO THE NEW TENANT

Dust flew from the broom
of a Pakistani mother
sweeping old carpets.
The lumpy brown couch welcomed
her and her husband,
and they stared at the TV
Mameleh claimed sent
dangerous rays to the brain.
In a bed soft with years
of restless sleep
this pair turned to one another.
The children they made
banged drawers
of the cherry wood dresser
where once photographs
from the Polish Pale
had faded to sepia.
Posed, the sisters linked arms
in a blazing summer field,
one escaping to America,
the others seized
for Auschwitz freight.
One day leaning out the window,
fingertips dusted with curry,
the children call: "Ami, come look,

36

an old woman is flying over Avenue J."
"She's in your dream of a crazy country,"
the mother answers them in Urdu,
buttoning a sweater over her tunic.
They all take bites of warm *chapatis*,
stir sugar for the tamarind tea.

MEDITATION AT PEAK SEASON

The competition
for calm is furious on the beach
where we bury our whims
only to dig them up again.

All day the uprooted move through the forest
toting blackened pots and infants on their backs.
Cattle bones dry in the sun.

Our radio music curves
arias of sea cows
mistaken for women
by full-blooded sailors.

Past the ratatat of bird or a gun, all day they move
past a river that surrenders swollen bodies to the shore.
Charred earth receives their chants of lament.

An ode to particles borne with each tide—
what we write on the sand as night takes small steps.
Bits of our singing stuck in our throats,
we poke at fires on the beach.

River fish hide in muddy shoals. Who dreamed
that the children would wave machetes in the church yard?
All day they move through the forest.

Once we were fish from a luminous split of the first cell
that harbored small odds of being pulled from our mothers.
Our ashes will blow out to sea that moans like a mother
burying her child.

UNLIKE MINDS

"God is not a mathematical diagram,"
Blake shouted, grappling with Newton's
insistence on reason.

The poet preferred cavorting
with cherubim and foolish virgins
in his garden.

What affects the apple affects the moon.
The vigil of science and the church
converted to dust while worms grooved

their path towards Sir Isaac,
inventor of the laws of motion
before naked Blake claimed he and his Catherine

were Adam and Eve when the pastor came to call,
and all conferred in the garden
of imagination with six-winged angels.

THE GRACIOUS DAUGHTER AND
THE MAN BY THE RIVER

When my minuscule self formed,
the wind rattled the windows, threatened
figurines of angels and saints.
In the same room, a half-finished bottle of Pommard,
and chocolate bon bons confessed to sins of gluttony.
Leather-bound books (embossed with gold),
saluted the arrival of a bibliophile-to-be. Soon, milky pages of
light would stream from my bassinet.

Walking by the river, my mother had come upon
a man naked in the leaves,
guessed that winds of chance had hurled him
from the sea as if he were Odysseus.
She noted smooth skin between patches of dirt,
offered him comforts of wine and a cloak.

"Why not stay?" her father asked, pushing back his chair
after a fine meal. He liked this stranger, their fluent talk of
food and books, and called to mind his unwed daughter.

"Are you married, sir?"
I am married to the church," the man rolled his eyes
heavenward. In a spasm of coughs,
my grandfather excused himself from the room,
took a swig of calendula tea to lull his nerves.

The priest urged the woman with wide gold eyes
to join him as he travelled north.
"We will gather documents of holy men
and philosophers," he whispered, dabbing his mouth with
a linen cloth.

His honeyed voice enticed her in Tours, Limoges,
Bordeaux, and in the capital where their moans
filled hollows in a summer storm. They lingered
over petits fours and cafe au lait.

My grandfather in the south would never be told
of my hunger for stories.
Neither the woman nor the man would be wed.

Moral: 1) Food and philosophy make for a heady mix.
Moral: 2) Women who want to marry should not take up
            with naked men discovered in the leaves.

AFTER I RIDE THROUGH
THE COUNTRY OF GRAVEYARDS

porcupine quills shoot out from the sun.
My childhood rows towards me in a creak of oars,
the buzz and murmur of hornets nesting in my legs.
Without sleep, I carried a bag of sadness,
my eyes screwed in above my cheeks.
Now in a dream I call out to the girl
I was when I sailed. The sun rows its red boat.
Racing her imagined twin on the wave soaked decks,
the child asks what keeps the sea from drowning the ship.
America shakes her yellow trees, a rain soaked city
in April. Sleep arrives in a gray silk bag.
Baku eater of dreams hasn't found my address.
Horses to race, Pillow White and Quiltie.
Today my chances crane their necks to see what unfolds
when I wave to the old porcupine sunning herself
in a field. A knot undone, sadness slips off,
gravestones in a hidden curve of that town I leave,
riding away from a blue dust of mouldering names.

THE INDIFFERENCE

of trees that haven't moved an inch
in our courtyard and seems to shrug

at the commotion of birds, dog ululations.
Hardly noticed is our crash into hours

which leave behind invisible villages
of the massacred.

What we can't see underfoot or in air
invades that half-sleep

where we grope in the rubble
of forgetting—names like nails hammered
to the wall, how to pry them loose?

We wake half-riddled with noise
on an island between two rivers.

Do east and west upset themselves
with how they rise?

Does the gunk and glide of what sinks
catch their eye?

This bland sky appears
to have put out of mind the red
of a lunar eclipse, or the rare occultation

of Regulus in Leo by Venus on October 1, 2044.
When we die I believe our consciousness will fly

like an ibis over the Nile, it will empty
loyal only to the sea.

ADIOSITO, MOTHER SNOW

Vamos. Enough.
The red sauce of the sun is hotting up
the sky as dawn fizzles out
like my baby-making eggs.

Snow on the zig-zagged roads, gray gutters,
vaya con whoever's in that Rolls,
silver-white like El Norte touching down
where the blue wind blows. Verdad?

What's in my futuro? Get me a reader
of palms. "Your mound's in Venus."
"Planet?" I ask. "Plan what? Ees no problem,
I see three kids."

Listen, my eggs are no-shows
and I'm not even Latina.
That "ez" at the end of my "In" name
comes from my padre's paramour

in the Sunshine State. Randyman. Long ago. Aye.
Call me Milagros. I got a lucky vida. Well, maybe.
Could be. Nobody's saying what it's like
to sleep under stones. Where have they been,

the ones who made me? Donde son?
Nice to see you, Mother Snow, tending to the rain.

MABEL, MERRICK, L.I.

The trucker took her on Sunrise
Highway as she crossed late winter, her
rust colored hair darkened with blood
in the snow. Late March carrying her away
in a flower filled hearse followed by
an entourage of mourners.

I remember her on prom night,
in a preview of her evening gown,
how she preened before the mirror,
auburn curls in an upsweep, arched eyebrows
startled at having turned so abruptly
from hollering tomboy to dewy girl,

bosom not quite filling the bodice
of a filmy green off-the-shoulder dress.
I'd hated her, the bossy older girl shrieking at me
for flubbing the ball in a backlot game.
She'd whizzed snowballs past my head,
wrestled with me,

pinned me down in the dirt,
sassed back her mother, her father.
All that howling on her lawn like a squall
through the maple trees under whose roots
quiet earth stirred with larvae and grubs.
And then suddenly this gauzy Luna moth,
Mabel fluttering in the vestibule.

In a black windbreaker, hands jamming the wheel,
death roared through my dreams but stopped
when I raised my right hand to pledge allegiance
to dance at my prom when the calendar turned.

At the funeral I gave my upturned face to her mother's
wound of lipstick, a tired phrase slipping out
of my throat: God wanted her in heaven.
In some topsy-turvy afterlife I may tap Mabel
on the shoulder and salute her as one whose nerve
in battle I envied, a fierce girl soldier.

I'll ask how she transmuted into the dainty
princess floating through school, tagged by
dumbstruck boys
just before she did not look or was not seen
crossing on her bike in Merrick after WWII
when the war sick Johnnies came marching home.

THE GODSEND

The god of the ceiling takes note
of a solitary woman writing.
"Let me throw down some lines that will make her fearless
or make her weep. Then I'll spin out a husband for her
and get them an island so they can meet
in an old hotel on the path to the sea."

When they meet he lends them a leaky boat
and fish to catch. They stay afloat.
Later the god sends them a child.
"Oh, no, our child is falling
into the hole of its very first cry,"
the couple recognize the sorrow and weep,
faces red as sunset on the pebbly beach.

How to make amends? Peering through gray,
the god of the ceiling begins to scheme:
"Let me weave the wind with the sun."
Over days he tangles light and motion in a reverie of calm.

Choggah-rom, the marsh frog sings, *buzzu-zah,*
a colony of bees calls to its counterpart in a hive of stars.
Shih-hiye, reeds nod to the shore.
In strips of color love's anodyne
presents itself to the woman and the man.

"Name what you see," the god of the ceiling
coaxes them.
From their island they identify: *luna moth gauze-green,*
the gray yellow of a bird braiding its nest,
a cup of mud and moss
lined with tan grass, fish-silver mauve.

And the pair set sail for that purple line
of utterance at the outer edge of grace.
They find a story to write to the waves.
A godsend, they exclaim.

D.H. LAWRENCE CARRIES BAVARIAN
GENTIANS TO HER WALKUP AT DAWN

She quotes "slow, sad Michaelmas"
as she climbs the four floor walkup,
damp cum stuck to her thighs,
rust on the kitchen tub, hand spray, dangling,
and shuts off the memory of a boy
wrapped in sweet smoke, his sad need
not to have her stay with him.
When she calls the poet, Lawrence, to her side,
he praises her breasts, hard-nippled in the light
of the mini fridge, and places gentians
loosely in a yellow vase, "forked torch of the flower"
burning through September haze.
For him she splashes her secret parts
with cologne, the splendor of the sun bellying up
over the river and the city trumpeting
from earth walls in heat.

BACK WHEN ALL WAS CONTINUOUS CHUCKLES
(after a line by Anselm Hollo)

Doris and I were helpless on the Beeline Bus
laughing at what was it? "What did the moron
who killed his mother and father eat
at the orphan's picnic? Crow?" Har-har.

The bus was grinding towards Hempstead,
past the cemetery whose stones Doris
and I found hilarious. Freaky ghouls and skeletons.
"What did the dead man say to the ghost?

I like the movie better than the book."
Even "I don't get it" was funny.
The war was on, rationing, sirens.
Silly billies, we poked each other's arms

with balled fists, held hands and howled
at crabby ladies in funny hats, dusty feathers,
fake fruit. Doris's mom wore this headgear
before she got the big C which no one said out loud.

In a shadowy room her skin seemed gray
as moon dust on Smith Street, as Doris's house
where we tiptoed down the hall.
Sometimes we heard moans from the back room

and I helped wring out cloths while Doris
brought water in a glass held to her mother's lips.
But soon we were flipping through joke books
and writhing on the floor, war news shut off

back when we pretended all was continuous chuckles,
and we rode the bus past Greenlawn's rise
where stones, trumpeting angels,
would bear names we later came to recognize.

PATHS

White margins on the wing
    of the Ruddy Copper
feeding on arnica.
    She jots that down.
Next, a Buckeye but it won't stop
    long enough for her to inspect
forewing, hindwing, antenna shape,
    male and female differences.
On the pond her pink face drifts
    under a floppy hat.
Dazed, she drops and picks up
    her binoculars. Cicadas begin
practicing dulcimers and spectral lutes.
    Home, she records how far apart
and few those notes reverberate
    as days turn brisk.
She will write until evening
    flicks off its light
and the table withdraws to a corner,
    over it early autumn
    rifling through papers.
When she sleeps, a child
    will step into her body.
They will count Blue Morphs
    under a winter quilt.

EVE'S SOLILOQUY

When I was riddled with pizazz
and hot to trot,
gnats and mosquitoes didn't
bother me, after all it was heaven,
but now I'm past the middle
of that carrying on,
so long immunity.
Bugs bite
parts once sleek
as that trickster snake,
and still fair,
the blush of apples,
where curves quiver.
So says the mower
in our garden.
Adam gone soft
in the middle hasn't solved
the riddle of love
any more than I have,
pulls me by the hair,
wants his dessert
when I want mine
while time, bent and warped
in its space time event,
prepares to blow
the lights
of our tryst
with incalculable *pi*.

DOUBLE TANKAS FOR CHIANG CHING

Without remorse in
jail Mao's widow stitched up
dolls held by children
taught to scorn her. Their mothers
shouted die, demon-boned slut

when they heard Chiang's name.
Without remorse in chambers
of hell, one among the Gang
of Four, she spits at
Mao's phantom. Red Guards hiss.

GLAUCUS, THE FISHERMAN

Once he was a fish and dined with gods
in chambers of coral and rose.
Proteus and Neptune caressed
his silver scales.
Sea horses cantered
through jade-colored waves.
Now flung down on the beach
at dawn, he is fisherman
again and blinks at his paltry catch.
In pocked ochre light,
mermaids he dazzled dart away.
Rubble darkens the coast.
Triton's horn turns to rust.
The Whale weeps gray stars.

SYLVIA, ALOFT
(for my mother-in-law)

God and gravity
will not change
their laws of flight
to pull her back
to the window ledge.
Her lament is at an end,
gone with the blue wind
blowing past
the ailanthus
in a morning
that shrugged
its shoulders,
as if it were routine
to see legs
scissor into air,
a robe's pink blotch
dart downward,
followed by
a fantail
of waved hair,
flicking past
the kitchen windows
of neighbors
who were not looking
up or out,
and did not believe
in angels.

ON A DAY OF ELLIPTICAL MUSINGS

the roof wills us a puddle of rain
    with asymmetric edges
reflecting an iron fence
    and a rag or more of clouds

on their way to other comparisons;
    rust-colored, a Christmas tree put on its side
resembles a patient whose gut rumbles and sighs,
    that fence watches the light

as if it were scratched in a disappearing language.
    Does it matter if we sit
with heaped up plates of lamb croquettes
    or gnaw alone on bones of crow?

It's the same for the painter of ellipses,
    and parallel lines that meet or don't...
History hikes up its shoulders, tells its swollen truth.
    Best to stand in a field and learn what stars tell

of clocks. Long after we transmute who we are
    in a cosmic well,
far down the pike, time to lose its name
    like water lapped by the sun.

YELLOW GOOD-BYE,
TIME OF GRACE DENIED

A heat wave heavy with August
when she took sick. Fingernails
ridged, chipped, yellow-gray
like her matted hair, the limp ferns
draped on the window sill.

That yellow fleck in her viscous eye,
pink rimmed, took me in, knew
my fear and disdain as I backed away
from her iron bed.
Past the flies, fans muffled our voices;

whispering loss thick enough to cut.
Her yellow teeth in a glass,
urine stained sheets floated in a dream
of visiting hours.
"Good-bye," I saluted my cold queen.

She jerked her head away.
Bee fur light and torpor in the corridors.
An odor of Lysol and rubbing alcohol
fused in the room.
Beneath her muslin gown

stuck out cracked feet the color of tallow,
of candles blown out
through a gray haze of years.
That day collapsed into stammering night,
sounds of thunder, summer.

One-legged lightning ran in the sky.

MOVIE STAR LIES

We sat on the glider in the screened porch,
and M.T. Paterson who lived next door said
"You lied about Glenn Ford," her eyes hard as pins
on a map showing troop strengths on both fronts.
I'd forged "love" next to his signature
on the glossy sent from Hollywood.

"Under the magnifying glass any idiot can tell
it's signed in different ink." She licked her lips,
smug with the evidence. I said "I don't care,
he signed 'love.' You're not my friend
if you don't believe me." I swung faster on the glider.
Shoulders thrown back like a master sergeant,

M.T. marched out muttering "liar" under her breath.
Later, trying to patch things up,
I sent for a snapshot of Robert Walker
in uniform and slipped it under her door.
I decided the word "love" was too pie-in-the-sky.
With M.T. it was better to say "drool"
as in Troy Donohue makes me drool.

Once I let Glenn Ford step out of his photo,
coaxed him to sit down on our front stoop
and talk about *Gilda*, my favorite movie,

how his co-star really lived next door
in Beverly Hills and they chatted about golf
and hosing their lawns. "Yes, she's the one,"
he beamed as Rita Hayworth pulled up to our curb

in a silver limousine,
legs in black net slithering out the door.
"He can have that glamour puss," M.T. said as she gave
her the finger and waved them away
and we resumed flipping through the pages
of the latest *Photoplay*.

SOLSTICE AT YELLOW SPRINGS

Orange-tipped Sulphur
    your blithe course
through the July

of this Ohio grassland
    hey aye hey
mouse-eared chickweed

meadow rue, sassafras
    please us
as do Swallowtails

flitting through
    meadows
of bees in the asters

hey aye hey hornet hum
    Feverfew
Chickasaw Plum

HENRY VIII AND BASHO,
EACH IN HIS CENTURY

The king shakes his suppurating leg,
    pulls the bell—
in a residue of worn out songs,

valets carry away the royal
    piss, blood soaked
bandages, Henry's phlegmy rags. Snow rages.

Basho commits his brush to paper.
    Magisterial pines weighed down by snow,
birds rummaging, agitated print of their script.

    Subject to rules of crystal
snow bows to no man,
    not even a poet facing the wind
in a coat of woven straw.

GIRL OF PATAGONIA

Startling the dark of the *barrancas*,
she called *ayuda me*. Blinking, her eyes gathered

colors of the Rio Mayo at dusk.
She begged the scythe of the moon to cut her loose,

implored the mother of owls, pleaded with stones.
Summers ago near Perito Moreno,

the wriggling body pressed to her thighs,
was Mama's friend, a drunk ranch hand from Chubut.

What were the *canciones* she memorized from school
after he dropped her into the well with none to hear

her wail through the roar of the wind save a neighbor
who grumbled *puta*, latching the window, bolting the door?

The wind has stopped lifting her damp hair.
She has given herself to spiders

who brush her with their silk from a web of stars
in Scorpius—they chant her requiem.

POLONAISE

Our tenant, Marek,
dreams of Landowska
playing Scriabin, of strawberry
flowers starring a meadow.

Handsome Marek, pouring honey
into bowls of Rice Crispies.
Sunday. Monday. Does he hear me worrying?
Our musical Pole with binoculars.

When did it come last? Who will love me next?
My child pokes at *blinis* on her plate,
prints "Mrs. Marek" in a soft notebook.
"How does a man..." She points to her thighs.

The moon rolls in. Strawberry red.
Marek has spotted Mars.
"I write music of planet,"
he calls us to the yard.

Raging crickets near our red clay road
subside. Fall. Rain-soaked blue leaves.
Snow boots and connubial crows
leave tracks in the mud.

Marek finds a moon goddess
at a nearby mall. Strawberry lips
jabber and scold, "Music, music,
that woman and her child,

that's all you ever talk about."
Her secret fur is red, gamey as a fox.

"Look," I soothe my daughter,
"Marek stirs cream

in someone else's kitchen nook."
"Advertise for another man," she says,
poised to dust the piano bench.

PEGEEN, REAL LACE

Castle Irish, Pegeen,
time carried her sires
on a private train.

Peau de soie gowns
and Malacca canes
spoke of high style.

On the High Mass trail,
a convent haze of privilege.
Who remembered famines then,

that nightmare of the tribe?
Our Lady of Potatoes, forgive us
our Fridays, the mackerel-snapping

virgin girls.
Pegeen, was she sorely grieved
confessing to venial sins?

She couldn't bite her tongue
to quell the longing
and had her way with the intended

in the golf club locker room,
and maybe it was unseemly to flash
that satisfied grin as the band

played Galway Bay
and his Holiness, the Cardinal,
in carmine silk, bent towards her

as she sniffed his ring,
six weeks gone when she floated
up the aisle, the rite witnessed

by the spirit of a Sheila-na-gig
exposing herself in the carved
stonework of the church.

BORN TO AN AGE

that hugged Kate Smith, the rich mountain of her
        voice when I Lindy-hopped, hunted
and pecked an Underwood,
        looking for my name.

Mel Torme's signed photograph on my desk—
        I dwelled on the "sin"
in his *sincerely*, hot to love, frizzed curls
        I imagined under a wig

at the court of Louis XIV where I'd do the minuet
        to the beat of Lully.
When I found my mother's name, I traveled back
        to the first DULONG at dawn,

birds sounding the alarm, wolves eager to break
        the circle of fire.
My ancestor's amulet of claws warded off
        the dream-eating snake.

Over us a story was about to burst
            into the taking on of names:
*long goat, horn of moon, bison song, of the long
        markings of stars*, the tribe's gift to me.

When I exited, the elders were singing
        the sun awake, their arrows tracking forward
to velvety Mel and the lavish Kate
        in the land that stands beside her to the light from...
France? Was that my kissing cousin Olivier
        circling my thoughts in his coach and four
carrying a message from his century to the singing mountains?

LOVE STORIES

The man and the woman, soused
cry "rescue us" to their summer child.
She scrubs away their grime, tells them
they've frittered away their lives.

So they flitter away with promises
not to return. That child's bequest:
half-lies of time. It's the war. Nothing to do
but to swallow it whole.

Firepower ricochets from the border.
She serves, counts the dead,
more crosses in the field than lilies.
Clash ends. Blood-colored

streaks at the finch's throat,
orange glints on the river
when she swims toward fire and a naked boy.
A cloud throws back its barbed white hair.

Woozy years dance. She and the boy look
among the missing to be claimed.
Marriage won't redeem them.
Another war and lies their only child's inheritance.

DOORS

The tall school doors
you opened and closed
past the Pont Neuf
are still there.
Was it the old bridge
I crossed that day
earth opened to the mountains
and the hoopoe's song
above your stone?

When you entered his room,
did he look down the hall
before shutting the door?
In that house
did you float down the stairs,
your sweater, the blue
of summer nights
erasing patterns of water,
and prints of creatures
that hide from the light?

In another country
I left my footsteps in snow
gathered at your door.
You asked who I was
though I looked like him.

I saw your thinning
wren-brown hair and a gray sweater,
sprouting holes—dream doors
to bird houses, and storybook mice.

Your mouth tightly closed,
startled gold eyes asking me in.

THE DISAPPEARED

Dear Sister Paul's keyhole at which I kneeled
like a supplicant asking for answers
from her vanished hair,
the uncertain gender beneath her robe,

rooms where compass points spun, chalk wiped clean,
hypotenuse erased, and x standing for what sorrow
caused them to hand me over to others.
A shudder before the last rite.

My father has joined the order of dust.
I was the truth of my mother's secrets.
When I fingered her name incised into stone,
a defiant snail, bareback, traveled the arc

of what was not said by the mourners.
Dear wind, brace these sleepers in their passage,
buttress these bodies of dreams.

ANNE

Bells hurried us past room where nuns
combed out their secret hair.
Bells rang us into Vespers, and you,
shifting your knees, half-slept through

the *in nome patri fili...*
I wanted to loosen your braids,
bury my face in the cloud of their silk,
to tug at them like ropes on a ship.

Later when you let me loosen the bows, flaxen hair
wrapped your shoulder like a shawl.
I supposed your mother's body swaddled with linen
when they lowered her to earth, and our fathers,

prayed for at Mass, traces like our words in chalk
erased on hand held slates.
Arctic owls flew over the pole we twirled on the globe
in geography. Thumbprint small, our low country

tucked between Holland and France spun with the dirt
of that garden caked in your palm
when you dug out a stone I craved for its smoothness.
"My gift." You bowed from the waist like a courtier

in our history books.
I can almost touch the nubby blue of your coat
that winter Reverend Mother rested her hand
on your shoulder. "Children, this is Anne come to live

with us in the sight of God."
I try to recompose you, a fractured narrative
of small lips, long neck, square tipped hands.
After the war, I thought to write you, but what was

your family name? Dear Anne of Belgium,
once we scrawled our name on water, did you picture me
stirring a cloudy pond in America?
How I lived in another language?

Sometimes I see you peering in a mirror that keeps
your level gaze intact. I conjure you,
tall as the king's grenadier, a mother to daughters and sons,
and their children begging for stories.

LINES FOR AN AUTUMN PARTY WITH FRIENDS
(for Margot)

When I was born the Catholic Sisters claimed me
in the prefecture of Etterbeck.
Now your rooms hold me, friends unknot and embrace,

take me into their confidence.
We also celebrate what comes late in the year;
the theater of crimson in the tupelo, sassafras yellow,

willow, downcast leaves that weep green-gold.
It is our reward, these clouds piling up like gifts,
this light on the wine glasses and over the river

warming us late in the day when voices are a body
of exuberant music, and the sky lifts us
into a Queen of Heaven uncommon blue

soon tricked into fire—purple-red-and-mottled-gray—
fused above the palisades. We are lulled into supposing
winter will ignore the revelry, that cold won't come again.

FISH SONG

Once in a satori, an aha—I was wise
in that instant—a red fish leapt
from my ribs and circled the afternoon.
I lost who I was and swam, gills, fins intact,
my face wide-eyed, a bubble in the glass.

Today a red fish leaps out of a letter
from Maurice. Near Paris my cousin steps lightly
around and around in a house with a cat that claws
where the red fish sighs aha on a sleepy afternoon,
circling a half-dream of winter.

Maurice writes light disappears in the middle of the day,
that his hours are the same in snow, in rain.
He feeds the cat, the fish, finds what he needs.
I haven't lost who he is, his face,
the wide-eyed level gaze of my mother's kin

rise up to me when I dream. Blood of my blood, Maurice
and his family stories. He called me *cousine* Colette.
We would watch the *poisson rouge* in its glass house,
how it bubbled up to study us.

SAYING GOOD-BYE TO CARMEN

We're bumping along a strip of road somewhere
between Bergen and Lillehammer, fjords in rolling fog
unfold a complex opera of clouds:

"Isn't life...?" Did she say, "magnificent?"
Carmen, Carmencita, glints of amber in her eyes,
porcupine short hair.

It stinks, I thought but didn't say. The Fifties.
Girls hiking in Europe, we sang, hopped rides,
kissed boys, cadged smokes.

I searched for my mother; Carmen, for her mother
country. Toujours la la, slap-happy, what-the-hey,
don't cry, Carmen, spine straight as a flamenco dancer,

a contessa. Later, Señor Muerte in shadowy salons
snapped his fingers, clicked his heels, bowed out
with her husband, sister, brother,

not satisfied with the bounty of her parents in Peru.
Now Carmencita, seeming to wave him away,
proclaims a grace that insists like a line of song
long harbored in the brain.

Aye, Aye, canta, no llores.
Frail in a photo from Madrid, she is posed next to Pablo,
her middle-aged son. I almost see her shrug after she cracks

a joke, hear her voice hush as she conjures up
our old road days. Carmen, brave as a chanteuse
auditioning for a show she's told is soon to close.

I remember the *Canta no llores* of her *Cielito Lindo*, my alto
hugging the shore of that melodic line. Gray cells devour her,
mysterious workings muzzle her words, the bilingual *porque-*

because life bursts at the seams
of the skull and escapes in a clearing of the throat, an ahem,
an *aye caray, amiga*, Carmencita, *adios.*

SYLLABLES FOR A TRAIN WHISTLE

The smell of brown bananas soaked through paper bags,
a *get your ticket ready*, a hum, hush.
The mockingbird will master the *whoosh*
past fields of hay and corn.
A hedgehog hears this roar
as just another thunderbolt—
the roar of his Zeus.
Purple rain. Afternoon. What's in store?
All out for Philly and Baltimore, long gone.
Low moans grieve for six-pack burgs, crossing guards
and lumber stores. A cow out to pasture
was once an engineer loved by the gods.
Is there a story here?

I saw it first as an iron bull chawing
up my Belgian meadow. Nuns said not to call
attention to myself with sobs. Who did I think I was?
When I landed in America I put away that fear
along with my crucifix and rosary. Because of the Pope,
Catholics breed like rabbits, my new family sneered.
Sometimes I'd walk to the railroad tracks and wait
for metal boxes of people to rattle past.
Some showed a sign, a hand pressed to the window,
a blown kiss when I waved.
If it rained, I'd race under trees, lifting my face

to receive the splat of water on my tongue
as if it were communal wine in the name of the Father
whom I blessed for his knowledge of
if not consent to airy kisses from strangers.

COMPOSITE SONG

Our grandmothers composed
of fish, pond scum, crabs
and galactic dust

and their grandmothers
part ferret, meercat,
trace of red fox in their fur.

Light stole into their bones.
The darkness of those hours,
part shelter, part shield

as they slept, awakening
to the breath of danger in a wave,
beast, man, flame, spear.

The blind sun like Homer
reciting stories
listeners knew by heart,

of humankind, part trickster
lemur, part loyal dog.

PHOTOGRAPHS OF THE CHILDREN'S
INSTITUTE, BRUSSELS, BELGIUM

The cameraman's black and white shots showed
front and rear views, pale spaces
in the grass and trees.

In the pictures we were invisible yet the corners
had us in them. We were there when red poured
its blood of beets and communal wine.

At the railing, bread of the Eucharist
dissolved on our tongues. My knees dug into stone.
Stranded, I foraged for sleep the photographer

could not catch in his lens
any more than the scratch mark of curlews
above the North Sea.

The wind raked through me. I walked on sand.
Small damp hands scooped shells flung back to the sea.
So much for that gray-brown mumbled history.

Today the photographer's children roughhouse with their
dog. I blow them some kisses on the beach at Ostend.

SYSTEMS OF BELIEF

Landlocked, the ruler
    of Paraguay directed his ships
to sail from the coast. A will of God, he said.
    "God decreed us poor,

but we are rich
    in dictatorship." Insurgents schemed
to drown their chief.

    In Angleland of old, Canute
commanded the waves
    to stop. Is the king not god? The tide

advanced, he and his retine stepped back
    into dunes of oblivion.

Containing these benighted, the universe
    unfurls her sails,
sets out for the dark infinite,

where facts, like sailors lost at sea,
    dance the hornpipe of doubts
in one divinity.

FOR MY IRISH GRANDMOTHER

You would not have been cheered
by the facts of my birth—
misbegotten in a lowland country, a child
packed off to the nuns.
In lace jabot and pearls,
you would not have opened your door to me,

better to be plagued
by dreams of Celtic women buried headless
with spindles, hooded spirits and warrior virgins
of Armagh,

better to change yourself into a crow
like the goddess Morrigan,
or transmute to a red cow
blessed by Brigit, saint of milk and butter,

rather be named Sheila-Na-Gig,
Ireland's Venus of Willendorf,
gripping her pudenda in a Dominican friary,

or turn the children of Caitlin
into witches and warlocks,
like Medb, Queen of Connacht,
to protrude your tongue and bare your teeth
in Cavan Town or Westmeath—

Sweeney himself, roosting in trees
to mock the priests on their errands of mercy,
would applaud from his perch.

You, who groomed your first born for the priesthood
that God might go on blessing you with means
to give alms to the waifs of San Francisco,
to the ragamuffins of Fisherman's Wharf,
would not have opened your door to me.

"No better than she should be and after our money,"
you might have said of your son's love child.
Cast in your son's likeness, I write this poem for you,
grandmother, now buried alongside my priest-father,
the son you outlived by thirty years.

Favored be your seed and the blood of our tribe
that roiled with the French from Bordeaux,
and this lineage invading my shy Gascon mother to make
me kin.

EAGLES, MEDWAY PLANTATION
(Goose Creek, S.C.)

On the day Princess Margaret succumbs to a stroke,
we are afloat in rumors that the U. S. Government
will ship to the poor, some say backwater state
of South Carolina, a clutch of Taliban prisoners
to languish there making a sort of Guantanamo Bay
off the Back River, and our hostess urges us to write to
Strom Thurmond or to Allah himself
to reassure there is no *ahem*.
No one wants to pronounce that word
although it happens to local dogs snapped up by alligators,
to deer ambushed by coyotes, is what eagles ignore
this afternoon as they ride the thermals,
constitutes what Elizabeth Hyrne knew
burying her infant son,
and later in her diary: *January 12, 1704:*
"Was burned...out of all...I know not how in the night,"
also Thomas Smith after he purchased a tract of this land
from the Lord Proprietors, and before him,
eagle feathers in their hair, the Choctaw,
when they watchedthe English ships put into port,
bringing new kinds of *ahem*
with freight from that other world.

WINTER, BACK RIVER

It isn't the stream flowing south
    I speak to when I stand on the dock
but my old lowland polders pushing back

the sea—another winter to hold
    the skates I strapped on.
Ice, little fires and chocolate

before I was shooed home to vanish
    and reappear at court.
The Queen of Belgium from the Lunar

Sea of Bruges singles
    me out for travel through time
on the back of a swan.

We stumble on the country of
    Marie-sur-la-Lune
and her self-important rabbit.

Now I'm a traveller to the southland,
    far from North Sea snow and porridge.
When I peer through mist, Mary Mother's

light favors the rice mill at Pine Grove,
    and a rabbit sitting for its portrait.
What I look at is not what I see:

a map of childhood's meanders unfolds,
    and of this silvery back river,
the rise and fall of the tide.

GHAZAL FOR MARTHE

I give homage to my mother, the voyage
of my mother,

the edge of her solemn words, the stately carriage
of my mother.

The hive exhales the swarm, a barrage
of dust against the sun.

What is empty dies out, an unused language
to a mother.

A concoction of clouds, fallen and moon-ridged
on the river.

So it was written on the unread page
of my mother.

Conception in a hidden pod—a sage
expounds on birth and death.

Moonlit gauze of lunar moths over bones that cage
our mothers.

One season glides, blue ice, another rages
with fire and wind.

To keep their secrets from us asked courage
from our mothers.

Larvae tremble on a shadowy stage
of the teeming forest.

The mirage of her child sired in a dream was lodged
in my mother.

For Colette it transpired—wages
of beauty and light accrued.

With these *ahas* arrived a fragile knowledge
of her mother.

VISIT AT EVENSONG

Inside the church on the corner of Fifth
and Twelfth I said under my breath:
"I came only for the blue reflected
on the altar rail,
for the musky scent of lilies
and damp aisles, to say I'm the skeptic
who once saw Mary shadowed on a wall
of a third floor walkup on Tenth and Sixth."

"You are relieved of significance,"
she intoned. I strained towards her
but could barely hear. What else
she might have said wafted away
with the incense of my mother
mesmerized under her Holy Reverend dreams
and my wish for my parents to sing with me
"What Child is This?" in good voice.

CITY AUTUMN, THE 104 BUS

We read the windshield
wiper's monotone, accordion fold,
the bus door's song & wait for the light
to slip into green in front of the Dollarama.
On the corner LIQUOR blazes violet neon.
A merger: late-November-not-yet-winter.
Sirens release snakes of lament,
car horns mourn the stuck light.
Holiday garlands & markdown signs
shape the path through which we forge
our longings for the palpable world,
to love it intensely as we fumble
with keys to lock out the wind
upending umbrellas on Broadway.

READING DA LEAVES

what do you want
gimme a little something
before I start

you gonna write a lucky poem
that make you rich
in da dark I see big ship
you gonna meet this moviestar

I see in da leaves
you gonna have a long journey
in da fall da jackpot is yours
because of da poem

wait I see your poem on TV
you got a hit show
gods gotta make it right
gimme a little more

my mother got a bad heart
I can tell by your hand
you da kind of person
like to have fun with your brains

da moviestar is gonna love you
and you gonna read him da poem
but he has a bad heart

and has an attack
then you get an idea for this big poem
I don't have change for a ten
it's gonna be okay

ACKNOWLEDGEMENTS

Grateful acknowledgment is made to the following
publications in which these poems first appeared:
"Spinoza Doesn't Come Here Anymore" in *Boulevard*;
"Como Pantoum" in *Paris Review*; "Prison/Clouds" and
"After I Ride Through a Country of Graveyards" in
Salamander; "The Skeptic" in *Poetry After 9/11: An
Anthology of New York Poets*, edited by Dennis Loy
Johnson and Valerie Merians (Melville House Publishing);
"Elizabeth, The Rain" in *Smartish Pace*; "Courtyard Noises
from the North, Twenty Fourth Precinct" in *Urban Nature*,
edited by LaureAnne Bosselaar (Milkweed Editions);
"Stalking ee in the Fifties,""Paths" and "Cold Montage"
in *Chariton Review*; "Song for Fernand Léger" in *Indiana
Review*; "Two Kashmiri Poets" in *Black Moon*; "Spring
Offensive" in *Main Street Rag*; "My Priest Father's" and
"Eve's Soliloquy" in *Ploughshares*; "Rescue and Return"
and "The Disappeared" in *St. Ann's Review*; "After
Mameleh Leapt Out of the Window, Her Furniture Went to
the New Tenant" in *Antioch Review*; "Meditation at Peak
Season" in *Green Mountain Review*; "Unlike Minds" in
Drexel On-line; "The Gracious Daughter and the Man by
the River" in *The Massachusetts Review*; "Adiosito,
Mother Snow" in *Beloit Poetry* and *Poetry Daily; Summer
2000*; "Mabel, Merrick, L.I." in *Hudson Review*; "The
Godsend" in *Pembroke Magazine*; "D.H. Lawrence Carries
Bavarian Gentians to Her Walkup at Dawn" in *North*

Her Walkup at Dawn" in *North American Review*; "Double Tankas for Chiang Ching" in *Clackamas Review*; "Glaucus, the Fisherman" in *Caprice*; "Sylvia, Aloft" in *Brooklyn Review*; "Yellow Good-bye, Time of Grace Denied" in *New Hampshire Journal*; "Movie Star Lives" in *Western Humanities Review*; "Solstice at Yellow Springs" in *Pleiades*; "Girl of Patagonia" and "Photographs of the Children's Institute, Brussels, Belgium" in *Tin House*; "Polonaise" in *Kenyon Review*; "Pegeen, Real Lace" in *Connecticut Review*; "Love Stories" in *West Branch*; "Doors" in *Valparaiso Review On-line*; "Anne" in *Barrow Street*; "Composite Song" in *Poetry Northwest*; "Systems of Belief" in *Puerto del Sol*; "For My Irish Grandmother" in *US1 Worksheets*; "Eagles, Medway Plantation" in *The Progressive*; "Winter, Back River" in *Hotel Amerika* and *Verse Daily* (Prize Winner); "Ghazal for Marthe" in *Ravishing Disunities*, edited by Agha Shahid Ali (Wesleyan University Press); "Visit at Evensong" in *Monsarrat Review*; "City Autumn, the 104 Bus" in *Gulf Coast*; and "Reading Da Leaves" in *Woman Poet, East*.

The poet also thanks Charlotte Mandel, Wendy Ranan, Larry Rubin, Pamela "Jody" Stewart and Sarah Brown Weitzman for valuable suggestions in perfecting a number of these poems. Gratitude goes as well to MacDowell Colony, Virginia Center for the Creative Arts, Yaddo, Medway Institute, Millay Colony for the Arts and Hawthornden International Retreat for Writers for residencies affording cherished time to work on this collection.

ABOUT THE POET

Colette Inez is the author of nine books of poetry, including *Clemency*, *The Woman Who Loved Worms*, and *Getting Under Way: New and Selected Poems*. Her memoir, *The Secret of M. Dulong*, is forthcoming in 2005.

Inez was born in Brussels, Belgium, of French parentage and raised in a Catholic orphanage. At age eight she arrived in New York and was given into the care of a family on Long Island. She attended Hunter College and has lived in New York City most of her life. Inez is the recipient of numerous awards for poetry, including two fellowships from the National Endowment for the Arts, a Guggenheim Foundation award, and two Pushcart Prizes. She resides on the Upper West Side and teaches poetry at Columbia University.

The NEW YORK POETS SERIES *celebrates the strength and sweep of New York City's poetry community. It features the work of poets long-admired in New York and beyond for their development of a distinctive idiom and a unique poetic identity.*